Endorsements

This book is so relevant to our world today! The coaching is encouraging and easy to apply. I learned so much about myself through the activities, which allow you time to focus and process. The Stop to Think portion was a reflection point that encouraged me to dig deep into applying what I had just learned. I recommend this book as a game-changer to pivot your thoughts and grow!

Renee McKenney, CMP
Vice President
TripEvents
ITS

On the Go Coaching is an uplifting and encouraging guide. I love the practical, actionable ways for women on our journey to be inspired and energized. Thank you, Jossalyn and Stacey, for keeping it real in this perfectly timed affirmation. You are both powerhouses!

Pamela Ey, Ph.D.
Optimizes performance at the intersection of the
complex system and people doing the work

Are you a woman on the go with a desire to become the absolute version of yourself? Are you a leader, entrepreneur, or stay-at-home mom who needs to stay focused and get the job done? Do you want to clear away life's clutter and maximize your potential because you know that the world is counting on you? If you answered yes to ANY of these, then *On the Go Coaching* is definitely for you! Get started today and enhance your life forever.

Latricia Edwards Scriven, PhD
Pastor, Florida Conference of the United
Methodist Church

On the Go Coaching is a must-read guide full of powerful motivation for women considering their next move on their career path. It provides a space for readers to learn, reflect, and immediately apply through the power of journaling. As a woman who has made a big transition from education to corporate America, I enjoyed reading the authors' deep insights. I believe they will inspire women to increase their self-confidence and maximize their professional potential.

Crystal Wright
Learning and Development Manager

on the GO *Coaching*

30 Days of Life and Career Coaching for Women Making Moves

Stacey Joseph Harris
Jossalyn R. Wilson, MSOD, BCC

Publishing House

On the Go *Coaching*

30 Days of Life and Career Coaching for Women Making Moves

Harris, Stacey Joseph. Wilson, Jossalyn R.
On the go coaching: 30 days of life and career coaching for women making moves/ Stacey Joseph Harris and Jossalyn R. Wilson.
South Carolina: JT Publishing House, 2020.

ISBN 978-1-7341793-9-2 (paperback) – ISBN 978-1-7341793-6-1 (ebook)
Library of Congress Cataloging-in-Publication Data: 2021930480
http://lccn.loc.gov/ 2021930480

Printed in the United States of America
10 9 8 7 6 5 4 3 2 1

Introduction

On the Go Coaching is a working resource for the ambitious and ever-evolving woman. Whether you're an emerging leader finding your footing in the corporate space, a businesswoman with goals beyond the board room and a corner office, or a stay-at-home mom with your sights set on establishing a legacy that outlives you, this book is an invitation to start a 30-day learning journey.

Each day will present a new coaching target. We encourage you to press pause and become present with the coaching content and your thoughts. Don't quickly move to the next day. Immerse yourself in the reading and engage thoughtfully.

The coaching targets will invite you to dig deep and explore the answers within yourself. Embrace the necessary discomfort of awareness that leads to growth. You're worth the effort. There is a ***Stop to Think*** opportunity At the end of each day. These are embedded in the reading to foster reflection and self-discovery. After reflecting, challenge yourself to respond. Leverage the ***On Your Mark, Get Set, Go!*** application activity to transfer your learning into actionable items.

We are thrilled to take this journey with you over the next 30 days.

Make bold moves!

Your coaches,

Stacey and Jossalyn

Table of Contents

Day 1

Sweaty Palms and Buckling Knees

Do you remember your first presentation during a department meeting? Or, your first day on a new job? There's something about firsts that cause our hearts to race, our palms to sweat, and our knees to buckle.

The buckling is often paired with questions like, "What if I forget the pitch?" or, "What if I've bitten off more than I can chew in this new role?"

The first time may also give way to anxiety and fear. If we're honest, we've had the same feelings and questions on the second presentation or the third promotion.

Here's the truth about fear: fear is an immobilizer!

Fear makes assumptions.

Fear presents lies as truth.

Fear does not discriminate, and every opportunity to be brave is fair game.

So, how do you deal with fear?

Start by acknowledging that fear is not unique to you. Everyone experiences fear at different times for different reasons. It's normal.

Call it out! It's okay to say you're afraid. Give voice to the feelings you're experiencing. Your voice will help you to navigate your emotions better. Share your feelings with a friend, colleague, or partner. This step is also a great way to garner support.

Be brave and do it afraid (if you have to). Give yourself a pep talk. Remind yourself of other times you've managed your nervous energy but continued with completing the task. Recall your last victory and celebrate it again.

Make the courageous decision today

to face your fear and build memory muscle, so you're ready the next time your palms start sweating and your knees buckle.

Remember, you can do this!

What is making me afraid? Make a list.

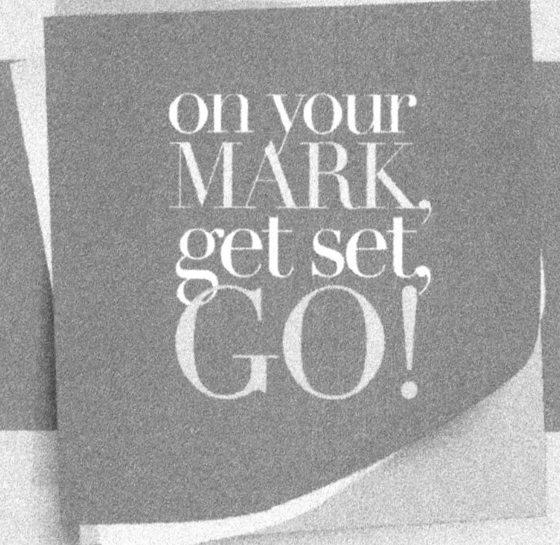

Review your list and commit to tackling one thing from the list this week. Acknowledge the fear. Call it out. Be brave and do it afraid.

Day 2

Finding Your Power

Caterina Scorsone's fictional character, Amelia Shepherd, in the highly regarded television series *Grey's Anatomy*, plays the youngest Shepherd child (family of 4), who witnesses her father gunned down at an early age.

Likely due to her life-altering experience, though never fully stated, her storyline reveals her fight with sobriety, irresponsibility, and devastating loss.

Despite her struggles, Amelia is a magnificent neurosurgeon. However, her ability to stand in her brilliance takes time, as she disqualifies herself from happiness and success.

Over time, the audience watches Amelia evolve. When she feels herself sinking, letting go of her power to overcome, she leans on her support group, accountability partner, trusted family members, and eventually herself.

Shepherd finds her power pose, with her hands positioned firmly on her hips, headed tilted toward the sky, and she "feels the sun!" She sees herself as a superhero, who can conquer anything, and that position gives her the confidence to keep going. Once she taps into her power, she's seen sometimes with others, but often alone, standing, "feeling the sun," believing in herself!

Perhaps Amelia's story is not your exact path. However, you've likely had an Amelia moment, moments where you overlook and discount your power—your ability to keep showing up, to keep going, or to continue the fight.

You are here because you have risen to the occasion.

You are here because you are powerful.

You are here because the world needs

your voice, the resolution that only you embody. Don't gloss over the tenets of your core. Living after loss, fighting through abuse, getting up after being kicked down, it took courage and strength to get up and keep going!

Stand up, sis!

Position your hands firmly on her hips, tilt your head toward the sky, and "feel the sun!"

You are a powerhouse!

What power(s) am I overlooking?

Journal about the systems you need to create or maintain to stand in your power. For example, craft daily affirmations or create an accomplishment log to remember winning moments. Then, identify your power pose!

Day 3

History Lessons

Blood and the fight for equality and justice color the stories of the Civil Rights Movement. From the Brown vs. The Board of Education ruling, ending racial segregation in schools, to the Montgomery Bus Boycott highlighting a heroine, Rosa Parks, refusing to give up her seat on a bus, which led to a year-long protest—these stories are painfully inspiring to recount.

Imagine those events shared by someone who lived during that time. History is the greatest teacher, and our history (the story of our past) offers lessons for today and tomorrow.

Two major events do not sum up the Civil Rights movement. Excluding the March on Washington and Dr. King's famous "I Have a Dream" speech would insult the person who walked miles to get there.

The same is true of your history, and taking inventory of your past is the way to secure your future. There may be parts of your story you'd like to forget, but yesterday's missteps can serve as a guide on your journey today.

Remember, the joy of victory, the pain of defeat, the anguish of loss, or the pride of reaching a seemingly impossible milestone — every experience has a blueprint for a learning outcome.

What will your history teach you?

No one knows your story like you. You have lived it. You own it. Your life is a textbook. The chapters within hold clues to help you now.

What moment of life has made me happy or sad?
Journal the experience.

Read the journal entry aloud. What history
lesson can you pull from the experience to help
you today?

Day 4

The Pinch Me Moment

In the middle of high-speed access, ongoing personal demands from family, and professional pressures, a quiet, still moment can feel too good to be true—a pinch-me moment!

Creating space for yourself is necessary. Prioritizing your needs is a priority. The notion that you can't pour from an empty cup is true, but you can't refill a broken cup either!

When we don't take time for ourselves, it erodes our culture over time, creating cracks in our foundation.

Explore and discover what brings you joy and rejuvenates you. Then, invest time, money, and uninterrupted mental space to refuel.

The residual impact will flow to those you desire to serve with your best and generate creative sensitivity to the work you are privileged to do.

Making time for you is not taking time from your responsibilities. Instead, it ensures you give responsibly through your actions, words, body language, and thoughts.

Pinch yourself and snap out of the "I am every woman" syndrome!

You deserve a break!

What do I believe about taking time for myself?

Plan an uninterrupted day or moment that brings
you joy and refuels you, then repeat often!

Day 5

Cracks in the Mirror

In 2013, Dove used a forensic artist in a beauty experiment to show how women see themselves. As he sat with his back turned to each participant, he asked a series of questions regarding their features and sketched the image he heard.

Afterward, the artist asked the planted stranger (an individual the organization asked to interact with the participant momentarily) similar questions to describe the same woman. Again, he sketched what he heard.

Having sketched both images, the artist asked the participants to review the portraits. The unveiling consistently revealed that the women were less complimentary and more critical of their features, while the stranger's description was kinder and more accurate.

Your self-image matters hugely to the story you tell yourself. Self-image affects the clothes you buy, the colors you wear, the jobs you go after, and how you treat your spouse, children, other family members, friends, and yourself. It impacts every area of who you are and how you respond in and to the world.

Generally, a cracked mirror is discarded as quickly as possible, as shattered glass doesn't seem to serve much of a purpose. Yet, artists use broken glass to create beautiful mosaics.

Alter the distorted image.

The job, the workouts, the clothes, nor your hair, define the light in your eyes, the dimple in your chin when you laugh, or the love people feel after hugging you.

You are the artist. Take your pieces, value their unique nature, size, form, color, and shape! Respect the difference in your pieces, as they are unlike anyone else.

Accept that YOU are beautiful.

A masterpiece!

What makes me beautiful?

Look in the mirror, stand tall, square your
shoulders, and compliment yourself every day
for the next seven days.

Day 6

Forget the Chair. Bring the Table.

Gender disparity in the workplace is old news. While some companies have made steps in the right direction to include women and assign value to the work (we've been doing all along), we still have quite a distance to travel.

In many instances, women have been pleading for a seat at the table, waiting for a chance to be heard, and praying for a promotion.

Fewer than half of women and men think the best opportunities go to the most deserving employees (Huang et al., 2019). From board rooms filled with older men to C-Suites that reflect the same demographic, it may take a different approach to have women consistently assume executive leadership roles.

What if you forget the chair and bring the whole table?

Bringing the table takes intention.

To start, here are five things you can do to develop your value proposition.

1) **Define your niche.** What are your natural strengths? Note: Taking the StrengthsFinder assessment may help.

2) **Keep a log of projects you've worked on or led.** Be sure to document your accomplishments and the support you've provided to your team.

3) Once you've defined your niche and tracked key projects and accomplishments, **develop a value pitch**. It may be a good idea to rehearse this pitch with a friend or colleague.

4) **Establish metrics for deliverables when possible.** Remember, the evaluation criterion within companies isn't always clear or straightforward. Get clear about what you do and have done. Assign value to your work with quantifiable metrics.

5) **Speak up.** I know this step may be a little uncomfortable, but this step is necessary. Talk about what you've done; don't scream about it. Be sure to acknowledge the help you've received along the way.

Position yourself as a valuable asset. Make people want to sit at the table with you, and if by chance no one shows up, take your table somewhere else!

How do I think my colleagues would describe the value I offer to the team in one sentence?

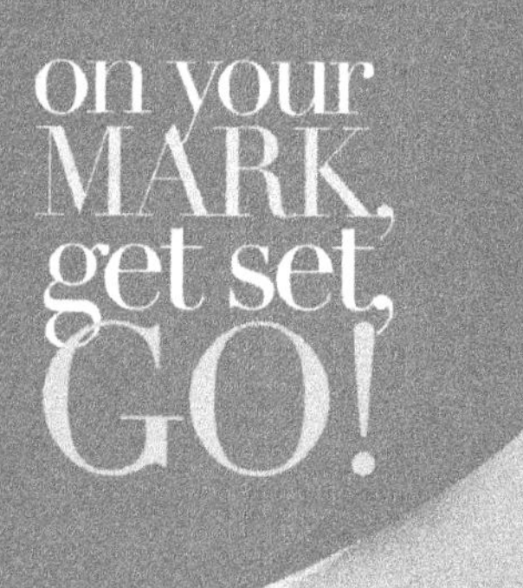

Reflect on the last project you worked on or led. Describe your contribution in one sentence. Do the two sentences align? If not, what's one thing you can do now to create value in your current role?

Day 7

Slingshots Go Forward Too

I didn't get the job!

The presentation didn't go well.

This relationship isn't panning out the way I thought it would.

The layers of life have a way of pulling us back. Sometimes, those experiences dare to appear isolated, disconnected, and absent of value—lingering as looming shadows over the vision we have for ourselves and our future.

However, shifting to an objective stance helps us make meaning—it helps us use what pulled us back to go forward.

The objective stance causes us to stand on the ball's offensive side and develop strategies to win. Allow what seemed to pull you back to serve as the catalyst that defines your winning strategy.

I didn't get the job, but I had an opportunity to practice my pitch.

The presentation didn't go well, but I gained new insights into adult facilitation.

This relationship isn't panning out the way I thought it would, but I've developed a new mental model of trust.

You have the psychological and emotional elasticity to use what stretched you back to propel you forward.

What experiences pulled me back?

Journal about your slingshot moment and
develop strategies that explain how you will use
that moment to go forward.

Day 8

There's No Shortage of Brilliant Ideas

Twenty years ago, Zoom calls weren't the method of choice for meetings, cryptocurrency was an emerging idea, and Pizza Hut and Dominoes cornered the market on food delivery.

A lot has changed!

Innovation is the necessary consequence of a changing world. If you're going to keep up with the pace of change, it will require you to tap into your ability to reason, create, analyze, imagine, and build.

But, if you think the "best" thing has

already occurred, then your mind will stop reaching for more. Simply put, there's no shortage of brilliant ideas.

It's time to unlock the creative genius.

What problem can you solve?

What idea have you been ignoring?

What are others still grappling with that you have mastered? Could the answer be tucked away inside of you?

Sometimes it's easier to wait for someone else to offer the solution. What if the responsibility to make the world better belonged to each of us?

We each have value to give to the world, but we must first believe that we have something magnificent within us to share. We must also be open to exploring our thoughts and innate abilities—allowing our imagination to breathe.

Use the following methods to get started. Establish a time for reflection. Mark off time on your calendar to sit with your thoughts daily, to train your brain to explore different paths of thought.

Use your journal to brainstorm. Articulate your thoughts on a specific topic or problem and see if anything special rises to the surface. Don't force it. Just let your ideas flow, even if they don't appear connected.

Rinse and repeat. Review your brainstorming notes and give a little more time to unpack the ideas that stood out to you.

Put a demand on your brain. Power it up. There's some good stuff in there.

Considering the happenings at work and home,
what problem can I solve?

Start brainstorming solutions this week.

Fill in the Space

Space left open, unoccupied, or unattended creates an open invitation for disruption. It is assumable, by connotation, that the act of disruption is entirely negative or hostile. However, disruption extends the opportunity for you to fill in the space.

Who you are and the talents, mindsets, and values you bring are unlike that of anyone else. However, the crowd sometimes has a way of making one feel like if they do not fit in, go with the flow, or engage in the same conversation—they do not belong (and maybe that's true).

The response you bring to disruption does

not exclude you from the room, the group, or the conversation. On the contrary, your disruptive response makes "accustomed to" uncomfortable.

Space-fillers are not placeholders. Space-fillers understand the depth, the height, and the width of who they are and what they bring. Therefore, by nature, they disrupt, making room for that which was non-existent!

Only confident people can be associated with disruptors because disruptors live in the unoccupied space. They see it and lean in. When we neglect to bring our full selves, we ignore the opportunity and the moment of innovation, creativity, and uniqueness.

Don't be unraveled by the silence.

Don't allow mediocrity to absorb your light.

Conception granted your permission!

Disrupt! It's not a cliché! It's an invaluable truth—YOU ARE ENOUGH! Fill in the space!

What space(s) do I need to occupy fully?

Stand in the mirror, and tell the woman you see,
"You are enough! Fill in the space!"

Then, create space-filler statements like, "My
question is valuable!"

Or, "My approach expands our belief that more
is possible from our team."

Your space-filler statements confirm your ability
to create meaningful disruption.

Day 10

Bouncing Back

Have you ever wondered how some women find their footing after great defeat and loss?

How did they manage to graduate with their master's degree while going through a rough patch?

What gives them the advantage when someone less qualified receives a promotion over them?

Their secret weapon is their resilient mind. These women have mastered the art of bouncing back in the face of adversity and unfavorable circumstances.

Life is sometimes unfair. The hand dealt isn't always the one we want to play, and quite frankly, sometimes the grass is greener on the other side. The challenge presents an opportunity to take your mind through strength training.

Here are three traits of resilient women:
1) **Resilient women train their thoughts to seek alternatives.** They see another path when others see the end. You can instruct your brain. You have control over your thoughts. Give your thoughts direction—tell them where to go!

2) **Resilient women embrace change.** Life simply doesn't happen in a straight line. There are often detours, rerouting, U-turns, and new paths altogether. You should expect it! You should expect that sometimes the only way that you can experience growth in your life is when things start to change.

3) **Resilient women know and believe they have options.** When one door closes, resilient women wholeheartedly believe they will be turning the knob of another door soon. They don't expect things to happen one way. Their approach to life involves problem-solving, reasoning, earnest

expectation, compromise, and opportunity.

It's not over; there's still time for you to win. Bounce back, girl! You may have to chart a new path, but new opportunities are waiting for you.

What recent setback or challenge have I experienced? Journal the experience.

Use the experience to list possible alternatives. For example, if you were turned down for a promotion, what are your options to move forward?

Day 11

Help! I Need a Life Jacket!

Ryan Cunningham wrote, "life jackets are designed to keep you from drowning in the water… yet millions of people on boats choose to go without [one]. The thought that having the life jacket in the boat makes you safe isn't good enough to actually keep you safe" (Ten Reasons Why You Should Wear A Life Jacket).

Life jackets are the lifeline, and they are essential to our survival because the day will come when the waters become rocky and we need help.

We can leverage our life jackets by using

G.R.I.T.!

G.R.I.T.:
> G-Get Support
> R-Relax
> I-Invest
> T-Track Your Stressors

Get Support

Get support by reaching out to family and friends who can help you improve your ability to manage the waves of life. Having people to support you stepping away, prioritizing, or redefining the narrative is essential. Taking a break, prioritizing what matters most, and telling yourself a different story about your abilities, helps your stance towards the internal and external work required to keep going.

Relax

Finding the time to rest your body and mind is essential when managing stress. Unrest often shows up in less productivity, missed deadlines, high emotions, and constrained reasoning. Sometimes we can feel guilty for taking this time, but we owe it to ourselves, our relationships, and our work to relax.

Invest

Time, like money, if not invested, is

wasted. Investing your time also helps you establish boundaries. It's easy to feel pressure to work 24 hours a day in our digital world. Have boundaries between work and home (i.e., choose not to check email from home or answer the phone during dinner). Develop boundaries that separate your worlds. Those limitations can reduce work-life conflict and the stress that tags along for the ride.

Track Your Stressors

Keep a journal for a week or two to identify which situations create the most stress. Record your thoughts, feelings, and information about the environment, including the people and circumstances involved, the physical setting, and your response to the scenarios.

Stress doesn't have to manage you! You can manage your stress with a bit of G.R.I.T.! Get to work; your stress-free future awaits.

What is impeding my ability to get support, relax,
and make investments?

Use a journal to track your stressors this week,
then devise a plan to get support. Incorporate
time to relax, and invest time and money (if
necessary) in areas that honor your priorities.

Day 12

The Dynamic Power of Not Now

"Yes."

"You bet."

"Sure, I will."

"Of course."

No matter how you say it, it's still a big fat YES.

We've all been guilty of being boxed in by our agreement. Saying yes to everything is the way to say no to what's important.

You might ask, "Why would anyone say no to the things that are important?"

The answer is clear. There must be meaning and value wrapped into yes. The quest for balance leads to the organic discovery of the purpose behind yes.

What if balance is not really about having the same weight on both sides of the scales? Achieving balance is not about saying yes to everything and getting it all done. Balance is more about assigning meaning to your yes.

Why should I say yes?

How does this align with the things that are important to me now?

The truth is, what balance looks like for the executive who is also a working mom and wife is likely different for the millennial professional who is single with no children. Balance is deciding what's important now and assigning a priority to it, and you're the only one who can define what balance looks like for you.

Again, the recurring question to establish priority is, "What is important to me now?"

Once you've identified what's essential now, simultaneously, you validate your yes. When asked to commit your time and energy, you can make an informed decision. The courage to protect your decision makes you accountable to yourself, and it may mean adjusting by removing some things from your plate. The matters you've deemed important or valuable deserve your attention—be accountable.

Remember, "no" is a complete sentence! If, by chance, you start to cringe at the thought of using the two-letter word, try "not now;" it will get the job done, too!

What are my responsibilities?
Make a list of all of the identified responsibilities. Next, consider the agreements you've made over the last 30 days (i.e., leading a team, baking cookies for the church, dog sitting for your neighbor, reviewing a grant proposal for a colleague, or driving your son's soccer practice carpool).

Take your list and assign a priority.

Go through the process of giving a number to
each priority.

1 – Most important right now; protect the item(s)
on my calendar.

2 –Somewhat important; delegation can shift to
someone.

3–Not now, I must have a conversation with
someone to adjust my agreement .

Given my responsibilities, where can I leverage
the power of "not now?"

Day 13

The Time is Now!

Marc Andreessen, co-founder and general partner at the venture capital firm Andreessen Horowitz wrote, "Every Western institution was unprepared for the coronavirus pandemic, despite many prior warnings. This monumental failure of institutional effectiveness will reverberate for the rest of the decade, but it's not too early to ask why, and what we need to do about it" (2020).

In many ways, problem-solving is a lagging indicator because the solution comes after the problem. Provide answers long before the problem emerges.

What answers have remained unexplored

and untouched within you?

What solutions have you not offered?

Choose to lean into your ability to create. Don't lag because others don't see what you do right away. Start now! Build today!

You could be the answer to a global pandemic. Your idea could end systemic injustices! You could have the answer to equitable access or produce something that keeps others from experiencing a problem later. Stop waiting until the crisis to act!

Give yourself more credit than showing up after the party. Lean into your idea and explore its reach. Test your hypothesis! Fail! Fail again, but don't stop. Start now, and keep going! You have more answers than you know, and your answers could be the ones we need, and in many cases, have been awaiting. After all, needs emerge to be met.

Your time is now! Get ready!

What thoughts have I left untouched or untapped?

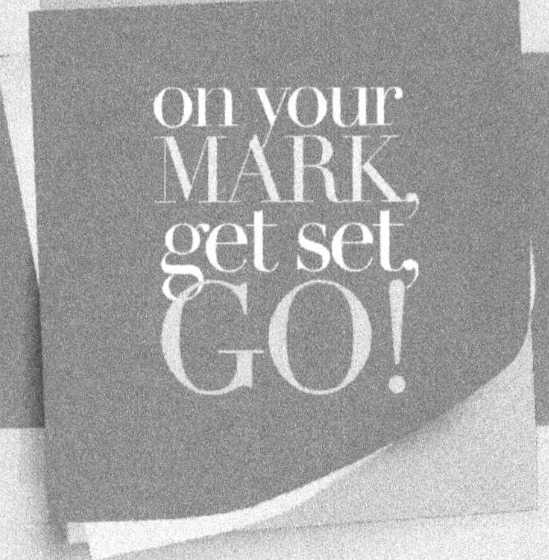

Choose one brilliant idea to dedicate time to this week. Make some traction with what you see in your head.

Day 14

I'm Listening. Tell Me More.

The opportunity to grow and develop personally and professionally often come wrapped with a bow in the package of feedback because quality feedback is a gift. Our ability to receive feedback and apply the knowledge gained is the gift we give ourselves.

Feedback can be positive or critical, and we need to hear and receive both. Positive feedback tends to land easily on our palate. The challenge comes when the feedback is critical.

Receiving the gift of critical feedback starts with distinguishing between who you are as a person and what you do. It's easy to internalize critical feedback as an assault on your character—however, great feedback targets specific behaviors. If you haven't made the distinction, the input can be challenging to hear. Remember, quality feedback intends to help, not harm.

Here are five tips for receiving feedback:

1) **Ask for feedback often.** Asking for feedback suggests that you welcome the information that will be shared. If you make it easy for someone to offer feedback, they will likely share more.

2) **Seek to understand.** Actively listen, ask questions when you need clarity on the feedback, and take notes during the conversation.

3) **Drop your defenses.** Try to relax. The person giving the feedback might be a little nervous too. Pay close attention to body language and facial gestures during the conversation.

4) **Manage expectations.** If the feedback recommends a modification in behavior, ask how they envision or see the change. It may also be worth your time to ask for a demonstration of the act if needed.

5) **Follow up.** This tip is significant. After the

conversation, reach out to a trusted advisor or friend and share the feedback you received. Ask if the feedback given resonates with how they experience you. If their answer is yes, their willingness to share will affirm the feedback and make it easier to digest. You'll also want to follow-up with the person who offered the viewpoint. Once you've started to apply the knowledge you received, ask for additional feedback on your current performance.

Feedback is a direct route to growth and development, so when you sit down to listen, don't be afraid to ask for more.

What positive or critical feedback have I received recently? Journal the experience.

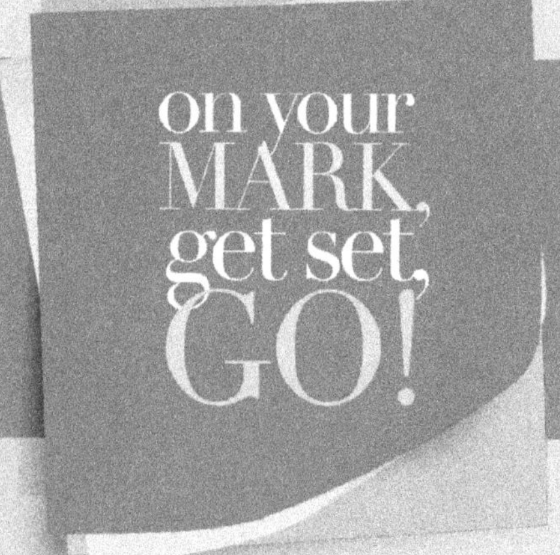

What feedback do you need to ask for now? Schedule a time this week to ask for the feedback you want.

Day 15

A Mountain of Possibilities

World-renowned businessman and Chilean mountain climber, Rodrigo Jordan, is known for building high-performing teams. After several quests up Mount Everest, Jordan decided to take a team to the top of Lhotse Mountain (the little brother to Everest, being the fourth highest mountain in the world) to celebrate their master climber, a seventy-year expert.

While he and his team had the lived experience of successfully climbing, they encountered a unique occurrence as the team reached base camp to determine who would go to the summit. Generally, the team started with training. Then, they started their trek, reached base camp, and assessed each team member to determine who continued to the summit. For Jordan (the leader of the group), he believed, as in times past, health, a person experiencing physical exhaustion, or seeing others die would play a factor in the decision. However, this time was different.

For this particular journey, once the team reached base camp, all climbers were in perfect health, and each climber wanted to continue the journey. Naturally, the team assumed Jordan would select the candidates who went ahead.

Initially, Jordan played the role the team expected of him. He started to think about who was in better shape, had the most experience, or the best configuration based on gender diversity. After spending time with each scenario, Jordan decided to do something different. He was brave enough to take the thinking to the group, and he proposed they determine who continued to the summit.

At first, the team pushed back because they expected Jordan to decide. Jordan struggled because he took old thinking to the group— meaning, he thought a specific subset needed to travel to the summit, as they had previously. Over time, a group member lifted a different thought, and the team eventually found a way for everyone to go to the summit.

The team went through processes and ways they had never considered before, but the answer resided in the group, and they realized how limited their perspective had become over time. While they grew in technical skill, it almost started to restrict their ability to remain innovative and see new possibilities.

Perhaps you have built paradigms mentally, relationally, emotionally, or spiritually that have started to limit your scope. Remember, possibility exists! Change often requires going through a space of discomfort. Remain open to being challenged and seeing opportunities that live beyond the surface. Use what you have (technical skills you've gained along the way), but stay committed to the possibility that more exists.

Climb your Mount Lhotse!

What possibilities am I missing because I've been unwilling to shift my paradigm?

Schedule a coaching conversation to unearth new possibilities.

Day 16

Look for the Ocean

If you're the big fish in your pond, it's time to look for the ocean. Our circle of friends, associates, and colleagues can become a comfortable place over time. Every now and then, we need to evaluate our circle.

Are we being challenged to grow?

Are the conversations provoking us to change?

Are we inspired by the daring moves the people in our circle are making?

Are we accountable for the goals we have

set?

Let's be clear; we need people. The people that get the first look at your personal development, decisions, and next steps are critical. Some of us have learned to keep our circles small, and by default, we have made the doorway to the center of ourselves narrow.

Sometimes, it's extremely crucial to open the door wide to allow the people you need in your life to enter. Transparency and vulnerability can be intimidating and awkward at first, but it gets better.

The first time you're in a conversation with a known millionaire, and you haven't earned six figures yet, you might become very uncomfortable. Some of the dialogue may be over your head. You may start to doubt why you're even in the room. By the second or third conversation, you've had time to google a few of the terms! The setting is likely still awkward, but you'll start to feel like if they can be a millionaire, then perhaps, "I can too!"

That's the beauty of the ocean. Ocean swimming can be intimidating, even for a skilled swimmer, because the ocean is a place for big fish. You'll never find a marlin twirling around on the shore; you'll have to go to where they are.

Deep sea fishing happens in the ocean.

Be open to experience something new. Success thrives in open spaces—new people, new conversations, new connections, new thought patterns, and new business models.

Remain open to the challenge of new relationships! Get out of the pond. You were made for deep waters!

Who are the top five people in my life?
What is their contribution to my life?
What value do I bring to their life?

Examine your answers to determine if it's time to find the ocean? What growth opportunity will you pursue this week? Consider growth opportunities that put you in proximity to other professionals.

Day 17

Value for the Process

In Positive Psychology research, appreciation correlates highly with increased happiness. While there are notable studies that show how appreciation increases performance and enhances culture, exceptions exist.

For example, Harvard Medical School found that "middle-aged, divorced women who kept a gratitude journal were no more satisfied with their lives than those who did not" (2011). Although contrary to previous research, their findings uncovered a truth that many of us face—appreciation sometimes does not always occur concurrently with our experiences.

Sometimes it's difficult to see the beauty

when you are in the moment because the scenarios do not foreshadow what's possible or what stands on the other side. To stand in the center of chaos, feeling cemented to the event, makes appreciation seem mythical. However, there are a few ways we can appreciate our journey.

1) **Slow down.** Slowing down offers the space to make meaning, which helps us make connections to the bigger picture. It allows us to zoom out and notice what's happening now.

2) **Counter the narrative.** We can show appreciation for the process by countering the story we tell ourselves.

3) **Review the expiration date.** Everything has an expiration date. If we review previous experiences we've overcome, we start to realize nothing lasts forever. That very notion reduces stress and the anxiety of the situation, knowing it will soon expire.

4) **Study!** Sometimes we sit in situations alone, not realizing the power of studying how others overcame or handled events they faced.

Studying the path of someone who has navigated troublesome waters brings gratitude to your heart because you realize you are not alone. You become aware of your ability to do something different.

The next time you face a challenge, don't give way to how you feel. Dig deep and express gratitude for where you are right now. You are uniquely qualified for the moment you are facing! Slow down, counter the narrative, review previous expiration dates, and study. The more you do, the more you will appreciate your process.

How can I show appreciation for and to my process?

Choose to change your language. Identify one thing you have complained about in the last 30 days and counter the complaint with appreciation. There's always a reason to be grateful!

Day 18

Secure Your Mask First

For years, flight attendants on airlines worldwide have been instructing us to secure our mask before assisting others. It's a lesson that transcends travel, yet most women tend to do the opposite.

Living in a perpetual state of busyness does not equal productivity or effectiveness. Overloaded schedules, social media notifications, and unmet needs are precursors to burnout and stress. Self-care is the superpower most women have not activated.

But what is self-care exactly? For sure, the definition is personal, but it's honoring yourself with the same care and attention you willingly give to others at a base level.

One way to tap into the superpower called self-care is to think about what brings you joy. Consider the things that cause a smile to emerge effortlessly or the experiences that foster calm and relaxation. These are the things that activate your self-care superpower.

Sometimes the journey to invest in your well-being is clouded by invalidated thoughts that suggest your actions are selfish. On the contrary, giving to yourself first ensures your ability to give to others. A rested, more settled, and happier version of you is a great gift to give to the people around you.

Self-care requires a commitment from you to yourself. For your commitment to be sustainable, self-care must be a daily priority, even if it means carving out 30 minutes a day for yourself. Give yourself permission to secure your mask first. You can't help anyone secure theirs if you're not breathing.

When was the last time I did something I really enjoyed that didn't involve helping someone else?
Did I feel guilty while doing it?
If so, what caused the feeling of guilt?
Journal the experience.

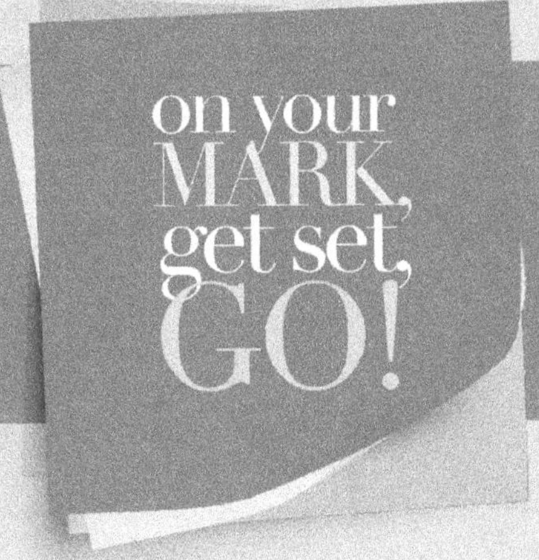

While looking at your calendar, review your commitments for the next seven days.

Allot 30 minutes of sacred time for yourself daily.

Write down what you plan to do during the 30 minutes (i.e., Bubble bath with music, quiet reading, get to bed a little earlier, go for an evening walk, or catch up on your favorite television show).

Day 19

Laughing Aloud, Crying Inside

Humor and laughter are and display more than a response to fun and games. They are used to present an alternative means of expressing arrogance, pretensions, criticism about injustices, or hypocrisies that can't socially (or legally) be expressed otherwise. Ultimately, the two present dynamic dimensions in their ability to bring one's truth to the forefront.

Humor and laughter remain versatile when it comes to disguising a level of discomfort, lightening a serious matter, or reducing the level of importance of a topic. In some ways, the pair present a cover-up. However, your thoughts and feelings deserve space and voice.

What causes us to use humor as an escape mechanism?

Admittedly, it's often easier to use laughter rather than lean into vulnerability.

Yes, some things are truly funny, and there are times when things are said in jest, but how you feel and what you think are not jokes. Don't use humor or laughter to cower away from your truth, and don't allow others to use humor to veer away from your point of view.

Laugh when it's funny but provide and own your perspective. Become comfortable with your words. Allow them to stand. Don't laugh aloud and cry inside—there's nothing funny about that stance.

What causes me to use humor or laughter to disguise how I feel or what I think?

Explore, record, and practice using statements that will help you resist the behavior to use humor or laughter to escape your thoughts, perspectives, or feelings. For example, while suspending judgment, I can acknowledge and dismantle the stereotypical remark; I do not have to laugh or go along with the comment for acceptance.

That level of acknowledgment could sound like, "I'd like to learn more about the comment you shared during today's meeting," which opens the door to a fruitful dialogue.

Day 20

Becoming a Money-Smart Woman

Women who control their money control their lives. Years ago, Kim Kiyosaki wrote a book titled Rich Woman: A Book on Investing for Women—Because I Hate Being Told What To Do. The title suggests that she urges women to equip themselves with financial education and establish financial peace and freedom through real estate investing, to take control of their money. How we manage our finances tells a compelling story about what's important to us.

To the spender, living equates to enjoying each day to the fullest. Acquiring new items offers a rush that makes each day worthwhile. This behavior could mean not giving much thought to the future. To the saver, putting every dollar away and watching it grow gives satisfaction and the feeling of stability. With great focus on the future, the saver may not give attention to daily pleasures. Whether you're a saver or a spender, you tell your money where to go and what to do. But, do you feel like you're in control? Are your financial habits serving you well? Are you living the life you desire?

Becoming a money-smart woman means:

1)   **You are honest with yourself about your financial standing.** Drilling down to the truth about your financial standing, how you reached that place, and where you want to be is key to developing a financial plan that supports the life you desire.

2)   **Learning about finances**. Start digesting all you can about finances. Tackle topics such as budgeting, credit, saving for the future, retirement plans, and investing. The knowledge you gain will empower you to make better financial decisions.

3)   **Establishing disciplines that support your financial goals**. Write out your financial goals and create action items to accomplish them. Start with a 30-day goal, then move to three months,

six months, one year, and so forth.

4) **Planning for today and tomorrow.** Achieving financial independence cannot happen without a plan. Studies show that women have a longer lifespan than men, suggesting that you'll need to cover more years in your financial planning. You may need to seek help from a financial advisor.

A money-smart woman is self-sufficient and free to make her own decisions. She knows what she wants, and she is disciplined enough to work for it—knowing the journey is worth it.

When do I recall learning my first money lesson?
Journal what you learned.

What money habits do you need to unlearn?
Establish a 30-day money goal to replace the old
habit and get to work.

Day 21

Strategic Conversations

Have you ever reacted in a way or said something you wished you hadn't? Most would admit they've had a moment they wish they could erase. Some conversations can get the best of us because we feel misunderstood, unheard, attacked, or belittled—all of which lead to unsuccessful after-effects.

When communicating, we give and receive multiple messages that extend well beyond what's spoken. Garnering your emotional fortitude can help you enter and engage in conversations with a different disposition.

Strategy requires discipline and a careful

approach. It's considering all of the pieces and orchestrating them such that you reach or exceed the desired outcome.

Perhaps you are up for a promotion and looking for ways to advance the scope of the work, maybe you need to have a tough conversation with your significant other, or you're looking for ways to bring together a group or a project, employ a strategy. Don't entangle yourself in conversations that aren't fruitful; stop to consider the pieces.

Ask for time to process the information you've received. Provide data to support your position. Listen with intention and develop your stakeholders' lexicon or those you connect with for the conversation. With a thoughtful strategy, you can and will see results.

Consider a conversation that didn't go well. What strategies could I have used to bring greater resolution?

Identify the emotional triggers that cause you to neglect your strategy in conversations. Use your awareness as a tool to monitor your response when communicating with others.

Day 22

Are We There Yet?

If you've been brave enough to take a cross country road trip with kids, you've heard the lyrics to a broken record they've sung (possibly echoed by an adult from time to time). With the passing of green interstate signs and mile markers, an antsy kiddo belts out, "Are we there yet?"

You know it's coming around again, but you're desperately hoping you'll be able to say "yes," before the question emerges. For road trips, there's a destination in your view, and you know when you've arrived. But in life, what if it's more about the journey than the destination. What if arriving is not the goal?

One way you start to embrace the journey is by becoming a life-long learner—a truth seeker, a knowledge junkie. The world keeps changing, so there's always something to learn.

Refining your skillset while learning new skills that companies are looking for is smart. Engaging in a new hobby and trying something different keeps you sharp and relevant. It's not enough in an ever-changing market to know a lot about one thing. Expand your knowledge to remain marketable.

As the job market becomes more diverse and competitive, position yourself to keep up with the rapid pace of change. Remain curious and stay open to learning. That stance will create an opportunity for more connectivity and community. Finding a tribe of other learners can fuel your drive and commitment to continue learning.

So, are we there yet? For the lifelong learner, the question is, "So, where are we off to now?"

How do I learn best (reading books, listening to podcasts or audiobooks, watching how-to videos, or taking notes)?
Journal your response and explore your last learning experience.

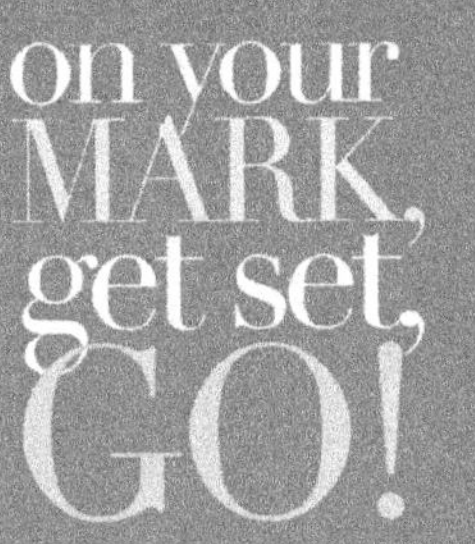

Develop a "Learn List" of topics, languages, projects you want to tackle before the end of the year.

Commit to three of the items on your list.
Happy learning!

Day 23

Google Me

Every now and then, you'll have a day or a moment that attempts to swoop in and deplete you of all joy, motivation, or belief. The moment you're up for a promotion, and it doesn't happen. Or, you're leading a meeting that doesn't go as planned or expected. Not to mention events or conversations that catch you by surprise in the middle of the day and completely alter or redirect the very linear path you'd carved.

Those moments, those days, have a unique way of subconsciously causing us to question our abilities, our knowledge, and sometimes our purpose. Enough of those days over a short period can masterfully package hopelessness and despair and ship them directly to your heart and mind's address.

Remain determined to keep yourself motivated despite the condition. When things don't go as planned, and you are wrestling with believing your brilliance or course-correcting your confidence, search for and replay moments when you learned or shined.

Leaning into personal moments of victory, ah-has, or learning is like searching the world wide web for ways to "understand who you really are."

You are solid.

Your knowledge can't be subtracted.

Read the articles in your repertoire. You are a BIG deal!

How can I encourage myself when moments or days don't go as planned or desired?

Google your name either mentally or in real-time! Become intentional about building and highlighting what you do and who you are to combat conflicting messages or beliefs.

Day 24

Selfies, Likes, and Shares

In the online world, everyone is an influencer, and likes and shares seemingly hold more value than the content of one's character. In many ways, social media has become the way messages enter the world. From social justice issues to grassroots campaigning—the reach is far, and the impact is powerful. What do your posts say about you?

Your influence belongs to you, and how you use it can inform, establish credibility, or damage your image altogether. Over the years, companies have adopted social media policies for employees to adhere to as a means to protect the company's reputation. If a company finds value in protecting its brand promise and mission, shouldn't you protect yours?

Tips for being socially responsible and safeguarding your reputation:

1) **Express your thoughts in a way that acknowledges your truth and respects others' opinions.** Everyone will not agree with you. They don't have to. It's really that simple. Once you post something on social media, it's not fair to get angry with someone for sharing an opposing view on your public post. If you want to share without judgment or comment, perhaps, you should consider sharing with family only. If emails and text messages can be easily misconstrued, imagine the damage done with 140 characters or a selfie without a caption.

2) **Your posts are history that can be recalled at a later time**. What story are you leaving for others to read? What will your grandchildren say about some of the things you post? Should you ever decide to run for office, can we trust your leadership if we only have your social media platforms? If you don't want it read ten years from now, perhaps you should think before you post.

3) **Don't forget the hiring manager is online, too.** Social media is the first stop for some hiring managers. Most people don't have their pages blocked, so it's generally very easy to find their content. Hiring managers look to see if the person on paper aligns with the online person. Also, if you should be working and your social media usage indicates standard work hours, that's not the best reflection of your integrity to remain committed to your work responsibilities.

Information is easily accessible, and there are countless opportunities for connection. When someone comes across your profile, make sure they experience the version of you that honors your brand promise and life's mission.

How do I want to be perceived online? Do my posts reflect what I want to portray?

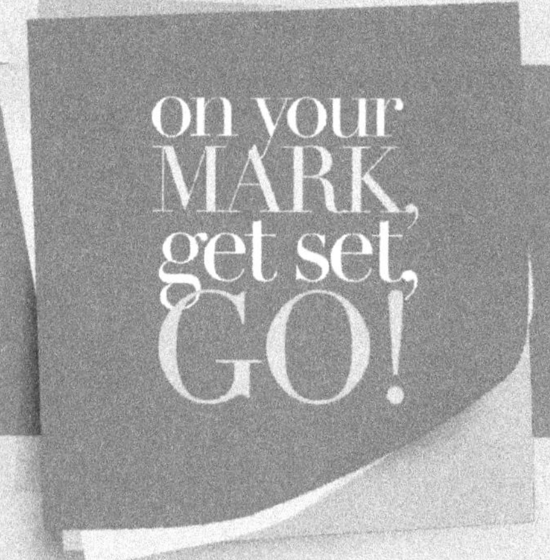

Using the Social Media Audit, assess your online accounts (LinkedIn, Facebook, Instagram, Twitter, Snapchat, and all other platforms).

Social Media Audit:

Review your last post on each platform.

Assign a word to describe the messaging
represented by the post.

Do these words mirror the online perception
you want? If not, what will you change moving
forward?

Dig Up the Roots

Social innovationists go through a process before actualizing their idea. They spend countless hours researching and analyzing the symptoms of the problem they aim to solve to ensure they attack root causes. Specifically, they name the top three symptoms stemming from the problem. Then, they ask themselves, "Why?" three times per symptom, at minimum. These entrepreneurs understand for change to occur and become sustainable, they must attack the root.

Likewise, when working to see changes in our personal or professional lives, establishing the goal and making ourselves promises is great. Still, our changes will likely fall short if roots are not tackled or addressed. Roots are often left unattended because it's easier and more comfortable to deal with branches—the symptoms or things we see on the surface. Symptoms don't go as deep, nor do they create complete disruption to our "business as usual" pace.

Getting to the root requires work. It takes self-reflection and commitment. However, once we uproot the old, we have an opportunity to plant new seeds, and you and those connected to you will appreciate the new blossoms. Pushing yourself to ask and answer your "why" may present a challenge and force true reflection, allowing you to move past symptoms and attack the root.

What roots do you need to deal with to understand the fruit you see in your life?

Don't allow another year, month, or day to go by dealing with weeds! Dig up the roots, plant vineyards, and experience what's intended for you.

What's really holding me back?

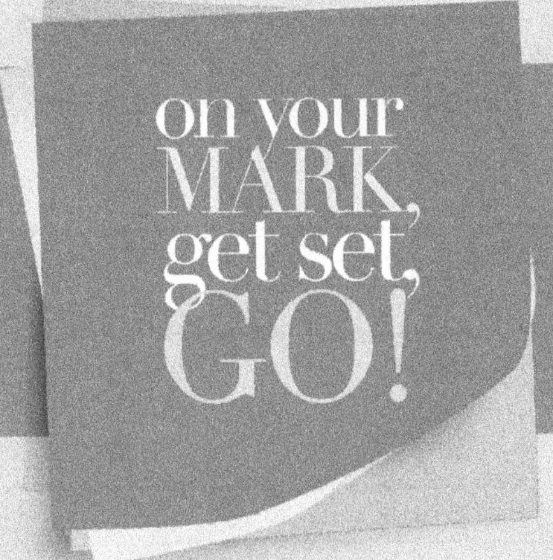

Perform a Root Exposure Assessmentä (REA) to
dig up the areas of your life that require change.

Root Exposure Assessment

The Root Exposure Assessmentä (REA) requires you to dig deep to uncover what is keeping you from your purpose. Be honest with yourself; expose the root so you can experience the change(s) you seek.

Root Exposure Assessment (Example)

Self-Awareness:
I realize I do not have the things I see for myself.
Symptom:
I don't finish things I set out to accomplish.
Why don't I finish things I set out to accomplish?
I lack discipline.
Ask yourself why: Why do I lack discipline?
I lack discipline because I've gotten decent results throughout the years and start to settle for those results being "good enough" for me.

Ask why again: Why are those "good enough" for me?
My results aren't terrible, so I sometimes believe the result I'm getting is likely all I can accomplish, and I don't see how continuing will shift what I'm getting or what's happening.

Ask why again: Why don't I see more opportunities beyond what I am getting?
I struggle to reveal that I don't have all the answers or know the path to my goal, and I don't always have "it" together.

Root Cause:
I struggle with being committed to a task because I know it will shift how I spend my time and demand accountability. I fear change because it will disrupt my previous patterns and behaviors. I am afraid to expose that I do not have all the answers, I am not perfect, and I do not have always have it all together.

Day 26

The Road Back to Peace

Everything is chaotic. Little fires are popping up everywhere, and you're the resident firefighter. Every big person and little animal around you need something. Calgon is not coming to take you away. Your peace has left the building.

The rumble of life is happening, and the roar of "what now" keeps your mind in drive when your heart desperately wants to pull over and park for a moment. If only you could exchange a moment of "doing" for a moment of "being" one with your thoughts and present with your heart—a moment of peace!

The doorkeeper to peace is your thoughts. What are you thinking? How are you managing your thoughts? Are the thoughts helping or hurting? The words that swirl around in our minds incite calm or panic. Pay attention to your thoughts. They are telling.

Peace happens within you. It's the calm within your heart that anchors you and guides your actions. Inner peace puts a muzzle on the noise of conflict and gives you just enough time to devise a means to get through it.

Peace helps to eliminate the need to control everything and everyone. Wayne Dyer talks about peace in a way that feels like our ancestors whispered a timeless truth in his ear. He says, "Peace is the result of retraining your mind to process life as it is, rather than as you think it should be." Being tolerant and accepting of things and people you simply cannot change guide you to peace.

Your wayfinding to peace is a self-guided tour through your thoughts and life experiences. Along the way, look out for clues that indicate you've entered a place of calm and clarity. Use the clues as a compass, and you'll always be able to find your way back to peace.

What does peace look like for me?
Journal your thoughts.

For seven days, take inventory of your thoughts
and feelings. Each day document your feeling at
the beginning and the end of the day. Use a   to
indicate a state of peace. Use an X to indicate

a state of frustration, worry, or overwhelm (if you're in any of these states, make a note indicating your triggers).

After seven days, evaluate your week.

What percentage of your week were you in a peaceful state?

Are you satisfied with your percentage? If not, what will you do to foster peace for the next seven days?

Day 27

Click Bait

Ever have a conversation about the new dress you'd like to purchase, but you're having trouble finding one in your size, the right color, and so forth? Moments later, you visit a social media site, and advertisement after advertisement contains dresses by companies you likely didn't know existed.

Naturally, it's easy to click the advertisements because you're searching for a particular item. However, throughout the week, you see more ads that appeal to you, and before you know it, you're clicking links, playing games, and buying clothes that you're convinced you want. You are bombarded!

A similar thing occurs when we are running low emotionally, spiritually, and mentally. When we are in search of something, it can become easier to take the bait. Clicking the bait might look like having unproductive conversations, staying in your head about the task you are trying to complete, or going further and further away from the quiet time needed to feed your soul.

The bait comes when we are tired, consistently frustrated, or overwhelmed. When the bait comes, sit with yourself. Feed your mind by taking an extended break. Disconnect the internet in your home for a day or two or silence your phone from notifications and calls. A healthy mind and heart can create healing and productivity internally and externally.

What bait(s) am I clicking?

Press pause! Identify where you are depleted
and intentionally recharge!

Day 28

Rainbows and Unicorns

Have you ever stopped to take in a rainbow or wondered if unicorns are real? Rainbows aren't typically seen every day; perhaps that's why we are so fascinated by them, and unicorns only show up in movies and cartoons, *or so we're told.* The rainbow and the unicorn represent "another kind," "other," and "different!"

Yet, we *ooh* and *ahh* at a sighting. We want to get a closer look because the difference enamors us.

As we get older, life happens, and we start to place more emphasis on "sameness." We like the comfort of fitting in, the safety of our bias, and the non-threat of our view of normal. If we aren't careful, we can use our words and gestures to shift or force others to fit into the boxes that make us comfortable.

Words are powerful, and gestures aren't always kind. Everyday insults grounded in stereotypes directed toward people within a marginalized group are microaggressions. Microaggressions can be painful and wound the human spirit.

Here are a few examples of microaggressions:

"So, where are you really from?" A question posed to a non-white person, assuming they aren't American.

Mistaking a Hispanic woman at a hotel for the housekeeper, assuming she couldn't work in another role or be a guest.

Why do you speak that way? A question posed to a non-white person implying the way the person speaks is wrong or incorrect.

Being aware that your bias has the potential to fuel your words and gestures is key. Pay attention.

If you are experiencing microaggressions in communal environments, there's an opportunity to educate others through honest conversation. Our differences are what make the world interesting. Embrace the texture and shade of who you are. Acknowledge and celebrate the shade and texture of others.

As a matter of fact, say it loud for everyone in the back, "Hello world, I'm a rainbow unicorn from *Otherville*. My colors are my superpower, and they are here to stay."

What biases do I hold or display?
Take some time to think and journal your thoughts
tomorrow.

Facilitate a conversation with a colleague or
friend about biases and microaggressions?

Solos and Duets

In the '60s, it was Sonny and Cher's "I've Got You, Babe," and Marvin and Tammi with "Ain't No Mountain High Enough."

By the '70s, Michael Jackson and Diana Ross were "'Easing' on Down the Road," and by the '80s Bill Medley and Jennifer Wells were having "The Time of [Their] Life."

These classic duets have not only won numerous accolades, but they have also penetrated generations and time. While individually incredible artists with extensive resumes, the results undeniably prove the power of collaboration, teamwork, and solidarity when the solo acts joined.

The power of collaboration and teamwork can be both advantageous and explosive when each member brings the best of who they are and what they have to offer. While the soloist's work is loved and respected, working together pushes and pulls you to go deeper and intentionally decide when to crescendo and decrescendo. It demands more and teaches lessons that sometimes can't be learned alone.

Learning occurs through connection—the connection of one idea to another, one belief to another. We don't arrive alone. It's the compilation of experiences and exposure that allows us to produce our best music.

Partner wisely, and thank your partners often. Who you are and where you are, was no solo act!

What partnerships have been most impactful to who and where I am today?

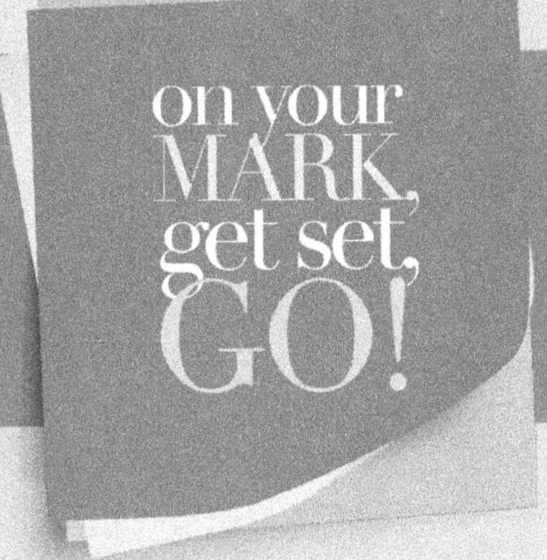

Show a form of gratitude to a partner who may not have realized their impact on your solo performance.

Day 30

The Enemy Called Inconsistency

"Oh, I'm sorry I'm late again. Traffic was a bear."

"I know I said I would apply for the position this week, but I never finished updating my resume."

"I know the proposal is due today; I will definitely send the proposal tomorrow."

"I'm not going to the gym this week. I'll start over next week."

Repeated actions are the ones remembered.

Take a moment to reflect. Do you notice a pattern of starts and stops? Are you constantly asking for an extension or giving a reason for not following-through on something?

Inconsistency is an enemy, not an ally. The effects of inconsistency can prevent you from accomplishing a goal or showing up as a polished and prepared professional, creating distrust with yourself and others.

One of the ways you can break this cycle of sabotage is to evaluate your thoughts and behaviors. When asked to take on a project, do you stop to think before you commit?

A minute of reflection will save much time and effort in the long run. A conscious decision to stop and evaluate what you have already committed to will help you determine if you can deliver on the request. This simple act will protect your reputation and help you to honor your commitments moving forward. Blindly saying yes is a recipe for inconsistency.

Is there an area in my life where I've been inconsistent? Take a moment to journal about it.

What behavior can I change this week to help me become consistent?

Stacey Joseph Harris

What is your coaching philosophy?

    I believe we are masterful beings loaded with creativity, competence, and courage. Sometimes our life and career experiences bruise these areas, and we start to second guess who we are, what we believe, and what we are capable of doing. Coaching provides an opportunity for partnership. This partnership involves a thought-provoking process that inspires action—establishing a safe environment for vulnerability and growth.

I believe coaching helps you clearly define your win by acknowledging where you are, where you desire to be, and the steps you are willing to take to get there. It challenges you to augment your potential and take control of your life. Coaching awakens the soul to what's been there all along.

What keeps you "on the move?"
Coaching women who are ready to step into the vast space that belongs to them keeps me on the move.

I also married the man of my dreams, and together, we spend time serving a community of people through Bible fellowship and mentoring. We are also fortunate to own a real estate investment company. When we aren't pursuing properties, I design beautiful spaces for my "heart" company, Wellspring Interiors.

I'm also on the move leading projects for a corporate entity.

When you "stop to think," what occupies your thoughts?

My mind travels back in time to reflect on God's faithfulness to my family and me, and my heart inflates with gratitude. I also consider legacy. I think about how I can continue a legacy of faith, family, and business started years ago by my grandfather and passed down from my parents.

When I "stop to think," I leverage my journal to archive my thoughts and write out my prayers. It's one of the ways I locate my heart and work my way back to the center when things are moving a bit faster than I'd like.

On the weekends, I "stop to think" about sassy shoes, a fierce handbag, and my next adventure with Mr. Harris.

Who should connect with you?

Individuals or organizations that are ready to do the work that coaching requires.

Where can people learn more about Stacey?
www.staceyjosephharris.com
www.facebook.com/staceyjosephharris
www.instagram.com/staceyjosephharris

Jossalyn Wilson
MSOD, BCC, ALP Certified

What is your coaching philosophy?

People are whole! Everything you need, you possess...no matter how you slice it, you've got the goods! However, sometimes we need a partner to help us navigate and explore what's possible, which actions to take to see progress, and the accountability to sustain the changes we desire.

I believe coaching facilitates movement from one state to another. It's a dance between self-awareness-who we are, process-how we show up and handle the "things" or spaces where we desire change, and task-what we choose to do to get results.

What keeps you "on the move?"
My husband and children keep me on the move! The things I desire to learn about them and do with them keep me actively aware of the gift of learning and connection, not to mention the partnership I'm able to have with my family, friends, and community.

Coaching individuals, groups, and teams in private, corporate, and educational sectors keep my mind and skills on the move, and I'm on the move learning and growing as a coach strategist.

When you "stop to think," what occupies your thoughts?
When I "stop to think," I think about the brilliance of God and the masterful nature in which He operates. It overwhelms and warms my soul. Knowing I'm found and seen by Him

brings me comfort and confidence.

I also spend a lot of time thinking about the social and systemic inequities in our world and my role in facilitating and creating resolve. I think about those things, sometimes specifically through my children's lens and the type of world I want them to inherit.

EVERY. SINGLE. DAY, I consider ways to maximize my impact, in the cutest and most comfortable flats, of course!

Who should connect with you?
Individuals, groups, or organizations ready for exploratory and expansive questions that bring results they can see, touch, smell, and taste.

People who want to publish a book or two should connect with my publishing company, and any momma helping her entrepreneurial kids live out their biggest dreams!

Where can people learn more about Jossalyn?
www.jossalynwilson.com
www.facebook.com/jossalynwilson
www.instagram.com/jossalynwilson

Andreessen, Marc, et al. "It's Time To Build."
    Andreessen Horowitz, 11 Sept. 2020,
    a16z. com/2020/04/18/its-time-to-build/.

Coury, Sarah, et al. "Women in the Workplace
    2020." *McKinsey & Company, McKinsey
    & Company*, 8 Oct. 2020, www.mck
    insey.com/featured-insights/di
    versity-and-inclusion/women-in-
    the-workplace.

Cunningham, Ryan. "10 Reasons Why You
    Should Wear a Life Jacket." *Beyond The
    Tent*, 23 Aug. 2019, www.beyondthetent.
    com/10-reasons-why-you-should-wear-
    a-life-jacket/.

Dove. "Dove Real Beauty Sketches." *Dove US*, 1 Nov. 2019, www.dove.com/us/en/stories/campaigns/real-beauty-sketches.html.

Harvard Health. "Giving Thanks Can Make You Happier." *Harvard Health*, www.health.harvard.edu/healthbeat/giving-thanks-can-make-you-happier.

CPSIA information can be obtained
at www.ICGtesting.com
Printed in the USA
JSHW031403040421
13211JS00002B/4